TONY BLAIR:

The Modern Prime Minister-Navigating a New Era of Governance and Globalization

William A. Lam

Tony Blair

Tony Blair

TABLE OF CONTENTS

Tony Blair

INTRODUCTION

Few individuals in British history have had such a profound impact on the political landscape of the country as Tony Blair. Blair emerged as a powerful influence as the 20th century gave way to the 21st, ushering in a new age of leadership marked by modernization, international diplomacy, and a reinvention of the function of government. "Tony Blair: The Modern Prime Minister" digs into this enigmatic statesman's life and times, charting his rise from impoverished beginnings to the pinnacle of power.

From Blair's early political career to his crucial position as the leader of the Labour Party and, ultimately, as the Prime Minister of the United Kingdom, this book gives a comprehensive study of his fascinating path. It analyzes his vibrant administration, which was characterized by bold domestic changes and an upbeat strategy for international relations that echoed throughout the world arena.

Tony Blair

We look into Blair's legacy using meticulous research, fascinating tales, and a critical eye. We dissect the intricate details of his ground-breaking initiatives, which revolutionized the economy, healthcare, and education, and we examine the moral and political dilemmas he encountered, particularly in light of the Iraq War. This book guides readers through the complex web of issues surrounding Blair's presidency while providing a comprehensive perspective of his achievements, failures, and the enduring effects they had on Britain and the rest of the world.

Through the pages of "Tony Blair: The Modern Prime Minister," we embark on a trip into the life of a leader who aimed to strike a balance between conventional values and the needs of a world that was undergoing fast change. This book serves as an invitation to consider the complex interactions between political vision, ideology, and the day-to-day reality of government. Join us as we explore the life, decisions, and legacy of Tony Blair, one

Tony Blair

of the most fascinating political personalities in
contemporary history.

CHAPTER 1: WHO IS TONY BLAIR

British politician Tony Blair presided over the UK as prime minister from 1997 to 2007. Blair, a Labour Party member, was born in Edinburgh, Scotland, on May 6, 1953. He gained notoriety within the party as a modernizing character and made a big contribution to changing its policies to make them more appealing to a wider audience.

Blair's tenure as prime minister was characterized by a dedication to a "Third Way" strategy that tried to blend parts of conventionally left-wing ideas with market-oriented tactics, as well as an emphasis on social and economic changes, notably advancements in education and healthcare. In the 1997 general election, he led Labour to a resounding victory, ending the previous 18 years of Conservative Party control.

Blair's choice to join the United States in the 2003 invasion of Iraq was one of the most contentious decisions he made during his time in power. This choice has drawn significant domestic and international criticism and is still under discussion and close examination.

Blair remained involved in world affairs after leaving office as prime minister in 2007, serving as a Middle East peace envoy and taking on different charity and business ventures. His time as prime minister had a long-lasting influence on British politics and policy, helping to determine the nation's course during a crucial era of transition and globalization.

1.1 Childhood

Early experiences in Tony Blair's youth were extremely influential in determining the course of his political career. Blair was the second child of Leo and Hazel Blair and was born on May 6, 1953, in Edinburgh, Scotland. His mother, Hazel, was an actress, and his father, Leo,

Tony Blair

was a well-known academic and lawyer. Tony spent his formative years in Durham, England, where the family later relocated.

Strong religious influences and a middle-class upbringing were hallmarks of Blair's childhood. He studied at Edinburgh's esteemed Fettes College, where he excelled in both academics and extracurricular pursuits. He showed his capacity for leadership while attending school by serving as captain of the school's first XV rugby team.

After Fettes, Blair went on to St. John's College in Oxford to pursue a legal education. When he was a student at Oxford, he started to get politically interested. He became a member of the Oxford University Labour Club and had a reputation as an engaging and intelligent speaker. Blair's love for former Labour Prime Minister Harold Wilson and his conviction in social justice and equality had an impact on his political views.

Tony Blair

After graduating from Oxford, Blair followed a legal profession, which strengthened his dedication to politics. He ultimately made the decision to change his direction and concentrate on politics, working as a lawyer and taking evening lectures at the Inns of Court School of Law. He won the 1983 election for the County Durham constituency of Sedgefield and was elected as a Labour Party Member of Parliament (MP).

Blair's early political career was distinguished by his initiatives to modernize and strengthen the Labour Party. He joined the centrist wing of the party and actively participated in internal party policy discussions. His ascent within the Labour Party was swift, and both party members and the general public were drawn to his compelling speaking style and strategic vision.

Tony Blair's early childhood experiences and influences prepared the foundation for his ultimate rise to power. The groundwork for the revolutionary political figure he would become lay in his upbringing in a family that valued education, his exposure to the legal and political arenas, and his zeal for social justice. The early years of Blair's life not only influenced his personal ideals but also gave him the tenacity and drive that enabled him to rise to the position of one of the most significant British politicians of his era.

1.2 upbringing

Tony Blair's upbringing is characterised by a synthesis of academic prowess, familial influences, and exposure to diverse realms that significantly influenced his political career. Some significant elements of his past are as follows:

1.Family and upbringing, to start: Tony Blair was raised in a very affluent family; his mother, Hazel Blair, was an actress, and his father, Leo Blair, was a prominent attorney and law professor. His parents' diverse backgrounds exposed him to a variety of experiences and viewpoints, which probably helped him relate with individuals from all different backgrounds.

2. Blair received his education at the esteemed independent Fettes College in Edinburgh, Scotland. His academic success as well as his participation in extracurricular activities and athletics demonstrated his leadership potential at a young age.

3. Strong Religious and Moral Values: Blair was raised in the Church of England, which gave him a solid foundation in these areas. Later, his devotion to social justice and his political views would be influenced by his faith.

4. Oxford University: Blair attended St. John's College in Oxford where he majored in law and was involved in politics. He switched from scholarly studies to political engagement when he joined the Oxford University Labour Club.

5. Legal Career: Following his graduation from Oxford, Blair briefly worked as a barrister. His legal training gave him strong analytical, persuasive, and public speaking skills that he would later employ successfully in his political career.

6. Entry into Politics: Blair decided to run for office because he wanted to have a real impact on society. Due to his eloquence, charisma, and ability to speak clearly to a variety of audiences, he joined the Labour Party and soon ascended through the ranks.

7. Modernising the Labour Party: Blair sided with the New Labour movement, which aimed to update and reposition the Labour Party in order to make it more appealing to voters. This required the party to abandon some of its more conventionally socialist positions and adopt moderate policies.

8. Parliamentary Career: Blair's formal political career began in 1983 when he was elected as the Member of Parliament (MP) for Sedgefield. He was able to develop

his political abilities and get insight into how the government functions thanks to his legislative experience.

Tony Blair's upbringing had these components, which gave him a special set of abilities, viewpoints, and experiences that were crucial to his ascent to become one of the most significant political personalities in British history. His tenure as Prime Minister and his lasting influence on the political climate in the United Kingdom were greatly shaped by his capacity to relate to various demographics and his dynamic approach to policymaking.

CHAPTER 2: POLITICAL RISE

His charismatic leadership, astute positioning, and dedication to reforming the Labour Party all contributed to Tony Blair's political ascent. Here is a summary of his political rise:

2.1 Early Political Engagement

During his stay at Oxford University, where he joined the Oxford University Labour Club and actively participated in discussions and debates on a range of political issues, Blair's political journey began. His zeal for social justice and his ability to speak well rapidly set him apart.

Tony Blair

Early political involvement by Tony Blair was the first step on his path to rising to prominence. A closer look at this period of his career is provided below:

1. Blair's interest in politics first surfaced during his time at Oxford University. He became a member of the Oxford University Labour Club and actively engaged in political activities, talks, and debates. During this time, he had the opportunity to hone his communication abilities and interact with other students who shared his political views.

2. Blair's love for previous Labour Prime Minister Harold Wilson had a major impact on the development of his early political beliefs. Blair's political thought was significantly influenced by Wilson's pragmatic approach to leadership and his aptitude for striking a balance between social and economic factors.

3. Political Rhetoric: Blair shown his innate capacity to influence others through his persuasive speeches even during his undergraduate years. His remarks frequently

struck a chord with listeners and demonstrated his potential as a magnetic leader.

4. After completing his studies at Oxford, Blair took a hiatus from politics to concentrate on his legal profession before joining the Labour Party. He quickly experienced a compulsion to return to political engagement, though. He joined the Labour Party in 1982 because he thought it would give him the best opportunity to make significant change.

5. Blair's early involvement in the Labour Party was highlighted by his activism and grassroots commitment. He actively engaged in neighborhood party events, interacting with supporters and developing connections with other party members.

6. Blair's political knowledge and oratory skills thrust him into the forefront within the Labour Party. He rose swiftly through the ranks and was commended for his contributions to party debates and policy discussions.

7. Blair's political career advanced significantly in 1983 as he won the general election in the Sedgefield constituency and was subsequently elected as a Member of Parliament (MP). His victory in the election signaled the start of his official political career and gave him a chance to promote his policy proposals on a bigger stage.

Blair's early political involvement showed his commitment to using politics to bring about constructive change. The foundation for his future leadership responsibilities and eventual ascent to the position of Prime Minister of the United Kingdom was laid by his capacity to clearly express his ideas, interact with a wide range of audiences, and find common ground with like-minded individuals within the Labour Party.

2.2 Election to Parliament

Tony Blair's election to the British Parliament was a turning point in his political career, catapulting him to the forefront of the country and charting the way for his future leadership positions. A crucial stage in laying the groundwork for Blair's ultimate rise to the position of Prime Minister was his transition from an Oxford-educated lawyer to a Member of Parliament (MP).

Blair's determination to bring about significant change was the driving force behind his decision to enter politics. He ran as the Labour Party's nominee in 1983 for the County Durham seat of Sedgefield. He made his formal debut in British politics during this general election. His choice to run for government was evidence of his dedication to putting his beliefs and goals into practice.

Blair's charisma, eloquence, and capacity for relating to voters were made clear during the election campaign. Voters were moved by his ability to communicate, and many were moved by both his vision for a modernized Labour Party and his own life narrative. He saw the necessity to modify the party's programs in order to better appeal to a larger spectrum of people as the socio-political climate changed.

Blair's official political career officially began with his Sedgefield election triumph. He brought with him a youthful vigor, an incisive speaking style, and a dedication to pragmatism as he took his seat in the House of Commons. His mix of qualities rapidly brought him acclaim from both party and fellow MPs.

Blair's time spent in Parliament gave him invaluable knowledge of how politics works, how negotiations work, and how difficult it is to put policies into practice. He made use of this time to become known as a formidable force inside the Labour Party and to gain a reputation as a practical and forward-thinking individual.

Blair's election to Parliament provided him with a platform from which to promote his policy proposals. It also paved the way for his eventual leadership of the Labour Party and, ultimately, his appointment as prime minister. In his later leadership responsibilities, his capacity to convert his ideologies into workable policies and his skill at forging alliances would be crucial.

In conclusion, Tony Blair's election to the British Parliament was a significant turning point in his political career. It symbolized the turning point in his dreams to change society into real action inside the halls of power. This action not only demonstrated his capacity to relate to voters, but also his dedication to establishing policies, modernising his party, and ultimately making a lasting impression on the British political scene.

5.3 Blair's ascension inside the Labour Party

Blair saw a swift ascent within the Labor Party. He allied himself with the party's modernising wing and pushed for changes in policy aimed at winning over more people. He served in a number of shadow cabinet roles while a frontbencher, giving him exposure to important policy issues.

Tony Blair

Tony Blair's ascent within the Labour Party was marked by his tactical vision, charismatic leadership, and the profound influence he had on the party's course. Blair's rise inside the Labour Party, from his early involvement to his eventual leadership, altered its identity and prepared him for his position as Prime Minister.

1. Early Political Engagement: During his time at Oxford University, Blair first became actively involved in the Labour Party. He became a member of the Oxford University Labour Club, where he developed his political activism, public speaking, and debate skills. His subsequent leadership within the party was shaped by these formative experiences.

2. The New Labour movement, which aimed to modernize and reposition the Labour Party on the political spectrum, was intimately associated with Blair's rise. He saw that the party needed to evolve with the times and widen its reach beyond its core support bases.

3. Blair's position as a moderate and centrist figure within the party found favor with many of its members and constituents. He was an effective change agent because of his capacity to strike a balance between economic security and modernisation and social fairness.

4. Blair's advancement within the party was distinguished by his strong involvement in policy talks. He participated in discussions about important topics like economic reforms, healthcare, and education. His persuasive arguments and aptitude for expressing difficult concepts in understandable words attracted support.

5. Frontbench Positions: Blair's ascent was accelerated by his selection to a number of shadow cabinet posts, where he gained experience in crucial policy fields. He was able to shape party policy through these posts and demonstrate his leadership skills.

6. Following the unexpected passing of Labour Party leader John Smith in 1994, Blair successfully ran for the

role of party leader. As he positioned the party as "New Labour" with a modern, fresh image, his election signaled a turning point for the organization.

7. A wide range of voters were drawn to Blair's leadership because of its electoral appeal. His engaging public speaking style and dedication to moderate ideals drew in both longtime Labour followers and voters who had previously supported other parties.

8. Electoral Success: Under Blair's direction, the Labour Party won the 1997 general election by a wide margin. With this victory, the Conservative Party's nearly two-decade reign came to an end and a new era of Labour control began.

As a result of Tony Blair's ascent within the Labour Party, the party successfully underwent a rebranding campaign to appeal to a wider spectrum of people. His capacity to forge alliances, speak clearly, and lead with a practical mindset laid the foundation for his later successes as prime minister. Blair's rise was a reflection of his profound awareness of the need for the party to change, which was crucial in reviving Labour and determining the course of British politics in the future.

2. 4 Labour Party Leadership

Following the tragic passing of Labour Party leader John Smith in 1994, Blair ran for and won the party's leadership position. As he positioned Labour as the "New Labour" option, one that was focused on modernization, moderate policies, and economic stability, his election signaled a turning point for the party.

The Labour Party under Tony Blair entered a revolutionary period that was characterized by modernization, rebranding, and a tactical turn toward the political center. Blair's aggressive leadership style during his time as party leader altered the party's reputation, programs, and electoral chances, leading to a historic triumph in the 1997 general election.

1. Blair's tenure was characterised by a deliberate effort to rebrand the Labour Party as well as by modernization. He aimed to transform it from its previous image and brand it as "New Labour," highlighting its modernity, pragmatism, and capacity for change. With this rebranding, the Conservative Party hoped to win over more voters, including those who had previously backed it.

2. Blair's leadership was distinguished by a break from conventional socialist policies. He supported centrist policies that struck a balance between social fairness and economic security. This "Third Way" strategy aimed to take advantage of market dynamics while continuing to focus on social justice and inequality issues.

3. **Electoral Strategy**: Realizing that expanding the party's appeal was essential to winning elections, Blair concentrated on topics that were important to the

electorate, such as crime, healthcare, and education. He developed a message that addressed the hopes and worries of common people.

4. Communication Skills: Blair's persuasive speaking manner and strong communication abilities were crucial to his leadership. He was able to communicate difficult ideas in understandable words and establish connections with a variety of audiences. This skill set helped him gain popularity and give the party fresh life.

5. Building a Broad Coalition: Blair's ability to lead the Labour Party depended on doing so. By appealing to both the grassroots and those wanting a more moderate stance, he was able to successfully unify the party's traditional left-wing forces with his modernizing program.

6. Policy Reforms: Under Blair's direction, the party adopted a new set of policies that favoured economic changes, advancements in education, and modernisation of the healthcare system. With this strategy, the party

hoped to continue its commitment to social justice while also meeting the practical requirements of its constituents.

7. Blair was aware of the role that the media plays in influencing public opinion. He made good use of the media, utilising his personal appeal and policy platform to promote the Labour Party.

8. Blair's presidency ended in the historic win in the 1997 general election, which put an end to the Conservative Party's nearly two-decade hegemony. Blair became prime minister after the Labour Party won a resounding majority in the House of Commons.

The Labour Party's prospects were revived under Tony Blair's leadership, and it was now seen as a serious contender to lead the United Kingdom. His ability to steer clear of ideological conflicts, forge alliances, and effectively communicate all aided the party's electoral success. Blair's contribution to modernizing the Labour Party's policies and creating a model for centrist leadership that reverberates in the party's subsequent approaches to governance are part of his legacy inside the organization.

2.5. Rejuvenation and rebranding

The Labour Party under Blair underwent a substantial rebranding drive. The party separated itself from its more traditional socialist beginnings and adopted a "Third Way" strategy designed to strike a balance between market-oriented policies and social justice. A larger range of voters, including those who had previously supported the Conservative Party, were to be attracted by this tactic.

A important turning point in the history of the Labour Party was highlighted by Tony Blair's rebranding and revitalization initiatives, which brought the party from the margins of British politics to the center of governance. Blair's effective leadership and subsequent ascent to the position of Prime Minister were greatly influenced by his strategic approach to reinventing the party's image and ideas.

1. Blair understood that the Labour Party's historical reputation as an extremist ideological party had hampered its appeal to a wider population. He aimed to reinvent the party as a cutting-edge force that welcomed change and responded to current issues.

2. Branding as "New Labour": Blair popularized the idea of "New Labour," which he used to describe his idea of a modernized and reenergized party. This branding denoted a departure from conventional leftist policies and a dedication to pragmatic, centrist governance.

3. Broadening the Appeal: Blair's rebranding plan was designed to win over supporters of the Conservative Party. He increased the party's appeal and electability by taking more moderate stances on topics like taxation, business, and social policy.

4. Emphasising Electability: One of Blair's main points was that for the Labour Party to make real change, it had to be in power. He highlighted the concrete changes it could make to people's lives in order to frame the party as a viable alternative to the Conservative administration.

5. Policy Modernization: The party underwent a dramatic policy makeover under Blair's leadership. Blair promoted measures that balanced social fairness with economic responsibility, reflecting a "Third Way" philosophy that appealed to voters in the middle.

6. Reaching Out to corporate: Blair's rebranding initiatives included interacting with the corporate world. This represented a change from the conventional Labour doctrine and shown a dedication to promoting stability and growth in the economy.

7. Blair was aware of the media's influence on how the public sees the world. He expertly used interviews and

media appearances to present the party's new image to the public and spread his message.

8. Blair's leadership successfully brought together disparate factions within the Labour Party, uniting the party. He was successful in bridging party differences and bringing the group together under a common goal of modernization and electability.

9. win in the 1997 General Election: Blair's efforts to rebrand the Labour Party culminated in a resounding win in the 1997 general election. With this victory, the Conservative Party's lengthy reign came to an end, making this event in British politics history.

The Labour Party's revival and electoral success may be attributed in large part to Tony Blair's rebranding and revitalization of the organization. A broad range of people responded favorably to his abilities to present a message of reform, moderation, and practical governance. In addition to redefining the party, Blair's strategic leadership helped to pave the way for his transformative term as prime minister and his lasting influence on British politics.

2.6 How to become prime minister

Strategic planning, political savviness, and a commitment to contemporary governance all came together in Tony Blair's path to becoming the Prime Minister of the United Kingdom. His election to the nation's top position was a turning point in British politics and prepared the way for his influential term as a transformative leader.

1. Leadership of the Labour Party: Blair's selection as the party's leader in 1994 marked a significant turning point on his journey toward becoming prime minister. His charismatic leadership, dedication to modernization, and capacity to unite the party around a common goal created the conditions for the rise of his party.

2. Blair understood the significance of expanding the party's appeal in order to win the election. A wide range of supporters, including some who had previously supported the Conservative Party, were drawn to his centrist views, dedication to practical governance, and rebranding initiatives.

3. *1997 General Election*: The 1997 general election was a turning point. A resounding win for Blair's Labour Party ended 18 years of Conservative control. This historic victory was made possible by the party's updated image, policy changes, and Blair's individual appeal as a charismatic leader.

4. New Government Formation: As Prime Minister-elect, Blair put together his cabinet and highlighted his top priorities for policy. He chose leaders who shared his vision and included both party veterans and newcomers.

5. Blair's first 100 days as prime minister were characterized by decisive action. His administration promptly got to work putting important policy reforms,

like constitutional changes, educational advancements, and healthcare modernization, into effect.

6. Foreign Policy and International Engagement: During his presidency, Blair's influence on the global scene increased. His attitude to foreign affairs, in particular his role in the Northern Ireland peace process and the Kosovo conflict, demonstrated his dedication to international diplomacy.

7. Blair's administration placed a strong emphasis on economic stability and explored measures to promote economic growth and job creation. The foundation of this strategy was the independence and responsible budgetary management of the Bank of England.

8. Blair's administration gave social reforms a high priority, including constitutional adjustments like devolution to Scotland and Wales. Initiatives to lower child poverty, enhance education, and modernize the healthcare system were also implemented.

9. Blair's tenure as prime minister has a significant legacy and an ongoing influence on British politics. During a time of fast change and globalization, his leadership style, emphasis on modernization, and strategy for international diplomacy helped to determine the course that the nation would take.

10. Blair's leadership wasn't without controversy, most notably the choice to support the United States in the Iraq War. Both domestically and internationally, this choice has been the subject of heated discussion and condemnation.

Tony Blair's ascent to the position of Prime Minister was evidence of his capacity to reform the Labour Party, garner a broad base of support, and articulate an inspiring vision for leadership. His innovative leadership style profoundly impacted British politics and showed how pragmatism, modernization, and international participation can influence a country's direction.

Tony Blair

In general, his political ascent was marked by his belief that a modernized Labour Party could win over a wide range of supporters. His climb to prominence was largely attributed to his dynamic leadership style, emphasis on communication, and readiness to modify party policy in response to the shifting political situation. As Prime Minister, Blair continued to influence British politics and carry out his plans for a "New Labour" administration that would balance social advancement with financial security.

CHAPTER 3: LEADERSHIP OF THE LABOUR PARTY

The Labour Party under Tony Blair underwent a dramatic ideological and policy shift during his tenure as leader. Blair sought to modernize the party and win over a wider constituency after being chosen as leader in 1994. His "New Labour" philosophy fused centrist, pro-business thinking with age-old social justice issues.

The party embraced policies under Blair's direction that placed an emphasis on economic stability, social welfare reforms, and public service enhancement, departing from its more left-wing roots. After 18 years of Conservative government, his leadership culminated in a resounding win in the 1997 general election.

His 2003 backing for the Iraq War, however, was incredibly divisive and caused rifts within the party and the general public. While he had electoral success, his term also spurred discussions about how to strike a balance between pragmatism and fundamental political convictions.

3.1 Important elements of leadership

1. Blair's leadership aimed to modernize the Labour Party's image by eschewing its "old" and more radical attitude in favor of one that was more moderate and electable. This required the party to distance itself from some of its established policies and appeal to a wider range of people.

2. Third Way" Politics: Blair promoted the idea of the "Third Way," presenting Labour as a party that struck a balance between conventional left-wing beliefs and market-oriented policies. With this strategy, social justice issues and the advantages of a market-based economy were meant to coexist in harmony.

3. Blair's presidency of the Labour Party resulted in an era of electoral hegemony for the party. After nearly 20 years of Conservative government, the party achieved historic success in the 1997 general election by winning a sizable majority in the House of Commons.

4. Economic Policies: Blair's administration carried out measures designed to sustain economic development and stability. They placed a strong emphasis on fiscal responsibility and public investment, which resulted in advancements in fields like infrastructure, healthcare, and education.

5. Blair's administration implemented a number of social welfare reforms, such as a minimum wage, investments in education, and welfare-to-work initiatives. These initiatives intended to boost social mobility and lessen inequality.

6. Blair's administration implemented constitutional reforms, which included the devolution of authority to Scotland, Wales, and Northern Ireland. In addition, the

Tony Blair

European Convention on Human Rights was
incorporated into UK law through the Human Rights
Act.

7. One of the most contentious facets of Blair's
leadership was his choice to support the United States in
the Iraq War in 2003. Significant protests and conflicts
over the choice were caused, both inside the Labour
Party and among the broader public.

8. Critiques and Legacy: Blair's legacy is characterized
by both admiration for his electoral triumph and
disapproval of the Iraq War. Some claim that under his
leadership, the UK underwent positive development,
while others assert that the Labour Party lost its
ideological focus and moved away from its historic
working-class base.

The Labour Party under Tony Blair's leadership changed
the course of the party and the larger political
environment, having a long-lasting effect on British
politics.

CHAPTER 4: PRIME MINISTERIAL TENURE

From May 2, 1997, until June 27, 2007, Tony Blair led the United Kingdom as prime minister. One of the longest-serving Labour Prime Ministers in history, he was a member of the Labour Party and won three straight general elections. During his administration, the Labour Party was modernized and a number of social and economic reforms, including advancements in healthcare and education, were carried out.

Blair's choice to back the United States in the Iraq War in 2003, however, is still one of the most divisive decisions he made while in government.

4.1 National Policies

The major domestic policies that Tony Blair implemented during his time as prime minister sought to modernize and enhance numerous facets of British society. These programs covered a variety of topics, including stability in the economy, social welfare, and healthcare. Following are some of the major domestic policy areas and projects during Blair's administration:

1. Reforms in education:
   - - Literacy and Numeracy Hours:To strengthen the fundamental abilities of young children, Blair's government established designated hours for literacy and numeracy education in primary schools.
   - - Sure Start: With an emphasis on young children's development, health, and wellbeing, the Sure Start program aims to offer early childhood education and support to families in underprivileged communities.

2. Healthcare advancements
   - - National Health Service (NHS) Investment: Blair's administration considerably raised spending for the NHS in order to shorten hospital

wait times, upgrade hospital infrastructure, and improve the standard of care in general.

- - NHS Direct: With the launch of NHS Direct, citizens now have quicker access to medical information and less need to rely on emergency services. NHS Direct offers a telephone and online service for health guidance.

3. • Welfare-to-Work initiatives

- - New Deal: The New Deal program sought to lower unemployment by giving unemployed people, particularly young people and those receiving long-term benefits, training, work experience, and assistance. It encouraged people to go from welfare to long-term employment.

4. Economic and social reforms:

- - Bank of England Independence: Blair's administration granted the Bank of England operational independence, enabling it to control interest rates and monetary policy. This action was taken to guarantee low inflation and economic stability.

- - Tax Credits: By offering financial help and encouraging employment, tax credits like the Working Families Tax Credit were introduced with the intention of assisting low-income families.

5. Constitutional Amendments:

- - Devolution to Scotland and Wales: Blair's administration supervised the formation of the Scottish Parliament and the National Assembly for Wales, giving both nations increased legislative authority and decision-making ability in fields including healthcare and education.

6. Reforms to criminal justice:

- - Human Rights Act: The Human Rights Act transposed the European Convention on Human Rights into British law and gave citizens access to domestic courts where they might pursue legal action to defend their human rights.

7. Diversity and social inclusion:

- - Minimum Wage: The establishment of a federal minimum wage aims to give low-paid workers fair pay and lessen economic disparity.
- - Equality Act: The 2006 Equality Act sought to promote equality of opportunity and prevent discrimination based on traits like age, disability, gender, and sexual orientation.

8. Environmental issues and energy:

- -Climate Change Levy: To promote energy efficiency and lower carbon emissions, the Climate Change Levy imposed a charge on energy use.

Blair's domestic programs demonstrated his dedication to modernity, social advancement, and financial security. While these policies sought to solve the myriad concerns that British society was confronting, they also spurred discussions and debates on matters like the function of government, access to public services, and individual rights. The legacy of these initiatives still has an impact on debates about governance and policy in the UK.

CHAPTER 5: FOREIGN AFFAIRS

During his time as prime minister, Tony Blair's foreign policy was defined by a blend of international participation, humanitarian action, and strategic relationships. His approach to foreign policy aimed to make the UK a significant role on the international scene while also tackling urgent global issues. Following are a few crucial facets of Blair's foreign policy:

1. Conflict in Kosovo:

- - Blair's participation in the Kosovo war proved how devoted he was to humanitarian action. The NATO air campaign against Serbia, which attempted to put a stop to ethnic cleansing and violence against ethnic Albanians, included a large contribution from the UK.

2. Peace Process in Northern Ireland:

- - In 1998, the Good Friday Agreement was made possible thanks in large part to Blair's strong participation in the Northern Ireland peace process. The deal was a crucial step in the establishment of a power-sharing administration and in putting an end to decades of sectarian warfare.

3. Integration into Europe:
Blair's administration aimed to interact with the European Union (EU) and contribute positively to the development of EU policies. He remained wary of several parts of European integration, such as the adoption of the euro, nevertheless.

4. Global Alliances and Diplomacy
- - Blair kept ties to the United States strong. President Bill Clinton and later developed a partnership with President George W. Bush. The UK's strong alliance with the United States led to collaboration on various international issues, including counterterrorism.

5. Middle East peace initiative:

- ●   - Blair engaged in efforts to advance the Israeli-Palestinian peace process. He played a role in organizing the 2000 Camp David Summit between Israeli Prime Minister Ehud Barak and Palestinian Authority President Yasser Arafat, though the summit did not result in a final agreement.

6. The Iraq War: Blair's decision to side with the United States in the conflict in Iraq continues to be one of his foreign policy's most contentious facets. The choice was made in light of intelligence suggesting Iraq had WMDs, however those WMDs were not eventually discovered. Domestic unrest and strained international ties were caused by the conflict.

7. Global Development and Aid: Blair's government prioritised global development and expanded foreign aid, pledging to fulfill the UN target of allocating 0.7% of the UK's gross national income to official development assistance.

8. Africa and Debt Reduction: Blair participated in movements for debt relief for developing countries and argued for more aid to Africa. An agreement to enhance aid and forgive loans for some of the world's poorest countries came about as a result of the Gleneagles G8 Summit in 2005.

9. International law and human rights: Blair's foreign policy placed a strong emphasis on international law and human rights. His government worked to advance human rights all around the world and backed the creation of the International Criminal Court.

Blair's foreign policy legacy is nuanced and contains both noteworthy contributions to peace processes and controversy, particularly with reference to the Iraq War, in addition to important accomplishments. His approach to foreign diplomacy and intervention demonstrated a blend of pragmatic involvement and a dedication to addressing global concerns, having a long-lasting effect on the UK's role in the international community.

5.1 Economic and social reforms

Tony Blair's government implemented a number of social and economic reforms during his time as prime minister with the intention of modernizing British society, fostering social inclusion, and promoting economic stability. These changes, which reflected Blair's goal of a more just and wealthy country, addressed numerous facets of welfare, economics, and governance. Here are a few significant social and economic changes made during his administration:

First, the **Minimum Wage**: For the first time in the UK, a national minimum wage was adopted in 1999 during Blair's administration. By ensuring that workers were fairly compensated for their labor, this program attempted to lessen income disparity.

2. **Reducing Child Poverty**: Blair committed to addressing child poverty and establishing goals to lower child poverty rates. To help low-income families, his

administration implemented policies including working tax credits and child tax credits.

3. Welfare-to-Work Initiatives: By offering training, job placements, and job search aid to people receiving unemployment benefits, Blair's New Deal initiative attempted to lower unemployment. It aimed to remove employment obstacles and place people in long-term employment.

4. Social Inclusion and Diversity: The European Convention on Human Rights was incorporated into UK law by the Human Rights Act of 1998, giving citizens access to domestic courts where they can pursue legal action to defend their human rights. Based on factors like age, disability, gender, religion, and sexual orientation, the Equality Act of 2006 sought to abolish discrimination and advance equal opportunity.

5. Education Reforms: - To help young pupils develop their core abilities, Blair's administration instituted reading and numeracy hours in elementary schools.

Families in underprivileged communities received early childhood education and support from the Sure Start program, which prioritised the health, happiness, and development of kids.

6. Healthcare Investment and Modernization: Blair's administration considerably increased spending for the National Health Service (NHS) to shorten hospital wait times, upgrade hospital infrastructure, and improve the standard of care overall. Access to medical information was improved with the launch of NHS Direct, which offered a telephone and online service for health advice.

7. Economic Stability: Blair's administration gave the Bank of England operational independence, enabling it to control interest rates and monetary policy. This action was taken to guarantee low inflation and economic stability.

8. The Climate Change Levy: The Climate Change Levy, a tax on energy use, was implemented by Blair's

administration to promote energy efficiency and lower carbon emissions.

9. Devolution: Blair's administration supervised the transfer of authority to Scotland and Wales, giving them more sway over issues like health care and education.

Blair's dedication to fostering a more equitable and inclusive society while simultaneously maintaining economic stability and prosperity was reflected in these social and economic reforms. While some programs were effective in tackling major issues, others drew criticism and generated discussions about the role of government in many facets of citizens' lives.

5.3 Global Leadership

During his time as prime minister, Tony Blair demonstrated global leadership through his involvement in foreign diplomacy, efforts to address global issues, and influence on the UK's relations with other countries.

Tony Blair

His leadership stretched beyond British boundaries and demonstrated a dedication to furthering the interests of the UK on the international stage as well as to fostering peace and solving humanitarian challenges. The following are significant facets of Blair's worldwide leadership:

1. Strategic Alliances: Blair kept up tight ties with Presidents Bill Clinton and, later, George W. Bush of the United States. His cooperation with the United States was crucial in addressing international problems including terrorism, wars, and economic stability.

2. Kosovo crisis: Blair's management of the crisis in Kosovo showed his dedication to humanitarian action. In NATO's air campaign against Serbia to stop ethnic cleansing and atrocities against ethnic Albanians, the UK was a key player.

3. Northern Ireland Peace Process:Blair's involvement in the peace process in Northern Ireland demonstrated his commitment to resolving disputes and fostering

reconciliation. A significant step toward putting a stop to decades of sectarian conflict was the Good Friday Agreement of 1998.

4. Global Development and Aid: The Blair administration committed to spending 0.7% of the UK's gross national income on official development assistance, up from the previous 0.6%. They also raised foreign aid. This dedication intended to combat poverty and advance sustainable growth.

5. Middle East Peace Process: Blair helped the Israeli-Palestinian peace process advance. Blair's participation in the 2000 Camp David Summit demonstrated his commitment to settling protracted disputes, even though there was no final deal reached.

6. Africa and Debt Reduction: Blair has promoted more funding to Africa as well as debt relief for poor countries. An agreement to enhance aid and forgive loans for some of the world's poorest countries came about as a result of the Gleneagles G8 Summit in 2005.

7. Human Rights and International Law: Blair's administration backed the creation of the International Criminal Court, which sought to hold people accountable for war crimes and human rights violations. His dedication to international law demonstrated his leadership on a worldwide scale.

8. Environmental and Climate Change: Blair encouraged conversations about the world's environmental problems and acknowledged the significance of solving climate change. He stressed the importance of international cooperation in resolving this urgent problem.

9. Anti-terrorism Initiatives: Following the terrorist attacks of September 11, 2001, Blair joined the US in the war on terrorism. He stressed the significance of intergovernmental cooperation in addressing global threats.

Blair's global leadership showed that he was prepared to take on challenging international challenges, promote humanitarian causes, and encourage international cooperation. While his administration was recognized for its accomplishments, it was also criticized, particularly in relation to the Iraq War. Blair's position on the international scene was a reflection of the difficulties and commitments that come with having a large following.

CHAPTER 6: IRAQ WAR

Tony Blair, who served as British Prime Minister from 1997 to 2007, was a key player in the Iraq War. The Second Gulf War, often known as the Iraq Invasion, or the Iraq War, lasted from 2003 until 2011. The United States started a military campaign against Saddam Hussein's administration in Iraq at the time, supported by the United Kingdom and a coalition of other nations.

Tony Blair's participation in the Iraq War was distinguished by his close ties to George W. Bush, the president of the United States. Due to the belief that Iraq may have WMDs and a possible connection between Iraq and terrorist organizations like Al-Qaeda, Blair thought that Saddam Hussein posed a threat. He claimed that removing Saddam Hussein from office was essential to advancing world security and halting the spread of WMDs.

The intelligence information Blair's government provided suggested that Iraq had WMD and could quickly use them. These assertions subsequently proved to be false, however, as no convincing proof of ongoing WMD programs in Iraq was discovered following the invasion.

The UK's choice to back the Iraq War was extremely divisive, sparking large-scale protests as well as conflicts within Blair's own Labour Party and the general public. Many attacked Blair for standing closely with the U.S., believing that the war was being fought to overthrow the current government rather than in immediate response to an existential threat.

The ground invasion followed on March 20, 2003, after airstrikes had started the military involvement. Saddam Hussein's dictatorship was overthrown rather quickly in the first phase of the war, but Iraq experienced instability, sectarian conflict, and insurgency in the years that followed.

Tony Blair

There were numerous repercussions from the Iraq War. Questions concerning the legality of the war and the decision-making process were raised in light of the lack of WMDs and the challenges encountered during the occupation. After the war, Iraq had years of unrest and violence, which aided in the emergence of extremist organizations like ISIS. The war also strained relations internationally and sparked discussions about the duty to protect and the function of military intervention in advancing world security.

Tony Blair's reputation in the UK was severely damaged by his involvement in the Iraq War. He was charged for deceiving the public and Parliament about the justifications for the war by many people. The Chilcot Inquiry, a thorough inquiry into the UK's participation in the war, came to the conclusion that the war was started as a result of faulty intelligence, poor planning, and overblown assessments of the threat posed by Iraq in 2016.

The Iraq War continues to be a highly divisive and complicated episode in world politics, with ramifications for the Middle East, worldwide security, and the standing of those who supported it.

6.1 Controversies

Several controversies resulting from the Iraq War are still being discussed and researched today.

1. Intelligence blunders The reliability of the intelligence that was utilized to support the war was one of the biggest points of contention. It turned out that the assertion that Iraq had WMDs was founded on flawed and deceptive intelligence. This generated concerns about the validity of the intelligence services and the veracity of the data given to the general public and decision-makers.

The second is "Regime Change vs. Security Threat" The idea that Saddam Hussein's regime represented a threat to international security because of its purported possession of WMDs served as the main reason for the war. Critics contended that the conflict was more about geopolitical goals and regime change than it was about preventing a pressing security threat.

3. Coalition formation and UN endorsement It was controversial to decide to invade Iraq without the UN Security Council's express consent. Many questioned the legality of the military operation and if it broke international law because there was no clear UN mandate.

4. Political and public opposition Massive political resistance and popular protests, especially in the UK and other coalition nations, were in response to the decision to support the war. The war, in the opinion of many, was unnecessary, and their leaders had not adequately represented their interests.

5. Humanitarian Implications There were many fatalities from the war, including civilian victims. Many people

decried the war's humanitarian effects, which included the forced relocation of people and the devastation of infrastructure.

6. Sectarian violence and destabilization Iraq saw considerable rebellion and violence after the invasion. Instability in the nation was exacerbated by the de-Ba'athification strategy and the dissolution of the Iraqi army, which led to an increase in sectarian tensions and violence.

7. Extremism's spread: After Saddam Hussein's dictatorship was overthrown in Iraq, there was a power vacuum that allowed extremist organizations like Al-Qaeda in Iraq, which subsequently transformed into ISIS, to flourish. These groups were able to flourish because of the unrest and constant conflict.

8. Repercussions on international relations Relationships between the US, the UK, and some of their longtime allies were strained by the Iraq War. The decision to invade and its effects on international relations were

criticized by nations that were against the war, such as France and Germany.

9. Legacy of Outstanding Business: Iraq was left with a frail and politically unstable nation after the final withdrawal of American and coalition forces in 2011. The ensuing development of ISIS and the ongoing difficulties with administration and security in Iraq have brought to light the complexity of the post-war environment.

10. Political Repercussions for Leaders: Leaders like George W. Bush and Tony Blair's political careers were negatively impacted by their participation in the Iraq War. Blair received criticism and demands for his accountability for the choices he made in the run-up to the war, and his popularity sharply plummeted.

These debates highlight the Iraq War's complex nature and its wide-ranging effects on international relations, regional stability, and worldwide security.

CHAPTER 7: LATER CAREER

Tony Blair has held a number of positions in both international politics and philanthropy after leaving his position as Prime Minister of the United Kingdom from 1997 to 2007. He accepted the position of Middle East envoy for the Quartet on the Middle East in an effort to advance regional peace.

The Tony Blair Institute for Global Change, which Blair also founded, focuses on themes like climate change, extremism, and governance. Additionally, he continued to be active in world affairs by giving speeches and offering advice to other leaders.

Tony Blair remained active in a number of positions and projects after leaving government as prime minister in 2007, which increased his influence after leaving office. His latter career included work in business, activism, peacekeeping, and international diplomacy. The following are some significant elements of Tony Blair's subsequent career:

1. Middle East Quartet Representative:
   - - In 2007, Blair was appointed as the United Nations, the European Union, the United States, and Russia's Quartet Representative for the Middle East. His goal was to advance regional economic growth and peace, with a particular emphasis on finding a peaceful solution to the Israeli-Palestinian problem.

2. Interfaith dialogue and the Faith Foundation:
   - Blair established the Tony Blair Faith Foundation in 2008 with the goal of fostering better communication and collaboration amongst many religious traditions. The foundation's main objectives were to promote religious tolerance, combat extremism, and create interfaith discussion.

3. Global health and philanthropy

- • - Blair took part in charitable activities, such as campaigns for world health. He founded institutions like the Tony Blair Institute for Global Change and the Africa Governance Initiative, which focused on everything from fighting extremism to governing in Africa.

4. Consulting and Business Attempts:

- • - Blair founded the Tony Blair Associates (TBA) as a consultancy that provided guidance to corporations and governments on a range of topics, including governance, investing, and the execution of policy. Discussions regarding potential conflicts of interest and transparency were sparked by his business endeavors.

5. Public speaking and book writing:

- • - Blair published a number of publications, including his autobiography "A Journey" and "My Political Life," which offered perspectives on his tenure as prime minister and his political journey. He also gave speeches in public where he discussed leadership and the state of the world.

6. Global leadership and governance:

- - Blair continued to participate in talks on global concerns, including geopolitics, global governance, and the influence of leaders. He persisted in pushing for practical and forward-thinking solutions to the world's problems.

7. Challenges and Disputations

- - Controversy dogged Blair's latter career. His involvement in the Iraq War was still under investigation, and his financial dealings came under fire for alleged conflicts of interest and a lack of transparency.

8. Policy Participation

- - Blair persisted in participating in policy discussions, sharing his opinions on themes like social inclusion, education reform, and the role of government in resolving international problems.

In his senior years, Tony Blair continued to be active in international affairs, advocate for interreligious dialogue, and work to advance peace and development. His extensive post-prime ministerial efforts made him a well-known international personality with a lasting influence on numerous industries.

7.1 International scenes

Beyond his political career, Tony Blair's influence was seen throughout the world. He sought to address urgent global challenges like conflict resolution, governance, extremism, and climate change through his different responsibilities, such as the Middle East ambassador and founder of the Tony Blair Institute for Global Change.

His influence on the worldwide scene was largely a result of his capacity to interact with world leaders, impart knowledge on global issues, and encourage dialogue.

7.2 International Impact

Tony Blair has had a significant impact on the world throughout his tenure as prime minister and into his post-political career. His influence can be seen in fields like world government, conflict resolution, and advocacy for a number of issues. Here are some of Tony Blair's most significant global influencers:

1. Diplomacy on a global scale

- - Blair's close ties to the United States. He was positioned by Presidents Bill Clinton and George W. Bush as a crucial ally in addressing global issues. His involvement in diplomatic initiatives like the Kosovo war and the Middle East peace process demonstrated his dedication to seeking peaceful solutions.

2. Middle East peace initiative:

- - Blair's position as the Quartet's Middle East Representative after serving as prime minister showed his commitment to ending the Israeli-Palestinian issue. He became involved to help the area achieve peace, stability, and growth economically.

3. Dispute Resolution

- - Blair's leadership during the Northern Ireland peace process, which resulted in the Good Friday Agreement, demonstrated his capacity for conflict mediation and negotiation. His dedication to rapprochement and fostering peace had an enduring effect.

4. philanthropy and global health:

- - Blair's charity activities in fields like global health and governance demonstrated his dedication to tackling important global concerns. The Tony Blair Institute for Global Change and other initiatives seek to advance effective government and inclusive economic growth.

5. Interreligious dialogue:

- Through the Tony Blair Faith Foundation, he promoted interfaith conversation with the goal of bridging barriers across religious traditions and fostering understanding in a multiethnic world.

6. Leadership and Advocacy

- - Blair's support for policies addressing climate change, poverty alleviation, and educational reform helped to keep him in the public eye as a global change-agent leader.

7. Thinking leadership:

- - Blair's publications, speeches, and other public appearances influenced thought leadership in fields like politics, international affairs, and the function of religion in contemporary life.

8. Enterprise and Consulting:

- He increased his influence through counseling governments and organisations on governance, economic growth, and policy execution through his consulting work and entrepreneurial endeavours.

9. Criticism and Controversy

- - Blair's influence was criticised for his participation in the Iraq War alongside the United States. Discussions regarding foreign involvement and its implications were molded by the controversy surrounding this choice.

Tony Blair's engaging leadership style, dedication to diplomacy, and involvement in a wide range of foreign issues have all contributed to his widespread influence. His activities, whether they were aimed at fostering peace, solving global issues, or promoting change, left a lasting impression on the political landscape of the world and continue to spark debates regarding his legacy and effects.

CHAPTER 8: LEGACY

Former British Prime Minister Tony Blair has left behind a sizable and intricate legacy that touches on all facets of British politics, society, and foreign policy. Blair's legacy as prime minister from 1997 to 2007 is frequently contested and assessed from various angles. The following is a summary of his legacy:

1. Blair's administration is renowned for its ambitious domestic policy agenda, particularly in the fields of welfare, healthcare, and education. In order to combat youth unemployment, his administration implemented programs like the New Deal, which also saw the adoption of the minimum wage and greater funding for public services.

Blair's administration also gave high priority to education reforms with programs like "Education,

Education, Education," which sought to raise academic standards and the quality of schools.

2. Economic Management: During Blair's administration, the UK's economy grew and was relatively stable. Throughout much of his term in power, his government maintained a conservative fiscal strategy that contributed to keeping inflation low and economic growth constant.
Many people view the choice to give the Bank of England operational independence in setting interest rates as a crucial step toward ensuring economic stability.

3. Foreign policy and the Iraq War: Blair's contentious choice to back the United States in its 2003 invasion of Iraq is intrinsically linked to his legacy. Numerous protests and disagreements were sparked by the decision both in the UK and around the world.

Blair defended the invasion on the grounds that Saddam Hussein had WMDs, despite the lack of evidence to support this assertion. Blair's legacy has been negatively harmed by the war and its aftermath, and he has received criticism for how he handled intelligence and his involvement in the battle.

4. Constitutional changes, such as the devolution of authority to Scotland, Wales, and Northern Ireland through the establishment of the Scottish Parliament and the Welsh Assembly, were overseen by Blair's administration. These adjustments were made in an effort to respond to persistent calls for more autonomy within the UK.

5. Impact on Society and Culture: Blair's administration promoted diversity and social inclusion. His administration introduced legislation, such as the removal of the infamous Section 28 and the equalization of the age of consent, to advance LGBTQ+ rights. During his tenure in power, the "Cool Britannia" movement, which praised British ingenuity and culture, also started.

6. Media and Communication: Blair's media-savvy strategy for politics and communication, known as "spin," changed how the public views politics and the media. The government's attempts to regulate messaging and presentation have drawn praise for their efficiency and condemnation for their misrepresentation of facts.

7. Blair participated in the negotiations of the Nice and Amsterdam Treaties and generally favored European unity. His attitude on the European Union, however, was not without controversy because he chose not to use the euro as a currency.

8. Legacy and Public Attitude: Blair's legacy continues to be extremely contentious. Supporters laud his attempts to combat social inequalities as well as his modernising of the Labour Party.

His involvement in the Iraq War, which tarnished his reputation and gave rise to claims that he misled the people, is the main target of criticism. His subsequent work as a public speaker and Middle East envoy furthered his complicated reputation.

Tony Blair leaves behind a legacy that is complex and includes both successes and disagreements. Discussions regarding his tenure in power and his long-lasting impact on British society continue to be shaped by his influence on domestic policy, international relations, and the function of communication in politics.

8.1 Political Influence

Through his pivotal role in remaking the Labour Party, his strategy for modernizing British politics, and his presence on the world stage, Tony Blair's political influence may be recognized. Here is a summary of his political impact:

1. Tony Blair is largely credited with modernizing the Labour Party and renaming it "New Labour." Under his

leadership, the party embraced more centrist ideas and distanced itself from its historical left-wing stances. This tactical change attempted to improve the party's electoral prospects by making it more acceptable to a wider variety of voters and eradicating its radical brand.

2. Election win: Blair's "New Labour" approach was carried out successfully, resulting in a historic landslide victory in the 1997 general election that ended the previous 18 years of Conservative control. His party's hegemony and his own standing as a political power were further cemented by his electoral triumphs in 2001 and 2005.

3. Blair's administration was renowned for its adept use of communication and media management, sometimes referred to as "spin." This strategy involves careful messaging and presentation to control the narrative and influence public perception. The manipulation of information in this strategy received criticism, but it also showed how powerful communication can be in influencing political results.

4. Blair promoted the idea of the "Third Way," which aimed to strike a compromise between orthodox left-wing beliefs and free-market ideals. This strategy intended to win over both traditional Labour backers and moderate voters by fusing social justice and economic progress.

5. Blair was influential outside of the UK due to his considerable contributions to international diplomacy. His intimate ties to the U.S. He gained prominence in world affairs after working with President Bill Clinton and President George W. Bush. His ardent support for the 2003 U.S.-led invasion of Iraq, which damaged his reputation internationally and sparked widespread demonstrations, also harmed his legacy.

6. Despite the controversies surrounding the Iraq War, Blair's administration supported humanitarian assistance where there were violations of human rights, as shown by their engagement in the Kosovo conflict. This position demonstrated a dedication to tackling global

problems and, if necessary, fostering stability through intervention.

7. Domestic Policy Reforms: Blair's legacy includes important changes to domestic policy, including the devolution of authority to Scotland, Wales, and Northern Ireland. He also brought in important social policies including the minimum wage and legislation defending LGBTQ+ rights. The development of British society and government was facilitated by these shifts.

8. After leaving government, Blair continued to influence others through his humanitarian work and his leadership of global organizations, including as the Quartet Representative to the Middle East. He continued to be active in a number of international problems while working to encourage talks between Israel and Palestine.

His remaking of the Labour Party, election victories, communication techniques, and involvement in international affairs all contribute to Tony Blair's political impact. Due to the Iraq War, his legacy is still debatable, although there is no denying his influence on British politics and international relations.

8.2 Leadership Role

Tony Blair's charisma, strategic thinking, communication skills, and capacity for overcoming difficult obstacles all distinguished his leadership style and job. Here is a summary of his position of leadership:

1. One of Blair's most distinguishing leadership qualities was his charisma and capacity for human connection. His dynamic communication abilities enabled him to persuade the public to endorse his vision for the nation and to successfully explain it. He was well-known for giving engaging presentations and being able to explain difficult concepts in a straightforward way.

2. Blair's leadership was supported by a distinct strategic vision for the Labour Party and the nation at large. His "Third Way" worldview sought to update the party's

principles in order to increase its viability while upholding its commitment to social justice and economic development.

3. Pragmatism: Blair's political pragmatism was a crucial aspect of his leadership. He was prepared to modify his opinions and policies in response to shifting conditions and public sentiment. He was able to increase the party's reach and win elections because to his pragmatism.

4. Global Statesmanship: Blair's influence transcended national boundaries. His involvement in foreign diplomacy, such as his work in Kosovo and his divisive opinion on the Iraq War, demonstrated his readiness to participate on the world scene and take on difficult global issues.

5. Blair's ability to manage crises was put to the test in the wake of the September 11 attacks in the United States, for example. He was able to act swiftly and reassure the populace, which was essential for preserving stability during these tumultuous times.

6. Media and Messaging: Blair's command of the media and messaging was a key component of his leadership. His administration adopted a media-savvy strategy, employing successful communication techniques to sway public opinion and control the narrative surrounding important laws and decisions.

7. Building Consensus: A key aspect of Blair's leadership was bridging political differences as well as those inside his own party. His ability to unite disparate viewpoints and cross ideological boundaries was a key factor in his election triumph and the accomplishment of his policy agenda.

8. While Blair's leadership was characterized by many positive qualities, criticism also surrounded his support for the Iraq War in particular. This action undermined public confidence and caused rifts within his party and among the general populace.

9. Blair's involvement in international affairs, public speaking engagements, and humanitarian activities allowed him to continue to exercise leadership after leaving office. He continued to play a significant role on the world scene, using his knowledge to add to conversations about peace, conflict resolution, and other global issues.

Tony Blair's charismatic communication, strategic thinking, pragmatism, and participation on a global scale defined his leadership style. He had a long-lasting impact on British politics and the global scene thanks to his ability to negotiate complicated political environments and deal with both home and foreign challenges.

8.3 Criticisms

Tony Blair's political actions and career have drawn a variety of criticisms from a variety of sources. Both during his tenure as prime minister and after leaving politics, he has received these attacks. Despite his major accomplishments, Blair was subject to intense criticism and controversy in the following crucial areas:

1. WMD and Iraq War Claims
   - One of the biggest and longest-lasting controversies in Blair's tenure was his decision to endorse the U.S. invasion of Iraq in 2003 based on intelligence that there might be WMDs there. Following the invasion, the absence of WMDs sparked charges of deceiving the public and causing regional instability.

2. Laws pertaining to civil liberties and counterterrorism
   - - The Blair administration implemented anti-terrorism laws like the Anti-Terrorism, Crime and Security Act 2001, which increased the scope of government detention without charge. The restrictions, according to critics, violated civil liberties and human rights.

3. Housing and government services:

- - During his term, Blair drew criticism for failing to sufficiently address the affordability of housing and the housing shortage. In addition, despite receiving more financing, some public services, such as healthcare and education, encountered difficulties.

4. Reduced Poverty and Inequality:

- - Despite efforts to lessen child poverty through programs like tax credits, critics contended that inequality still existed and that systemic poverty required more extensive solutions.

5. Public Finance and PFI:

- - Blair's administration adopted the Private Finance Initiative (PFI) to finance public infrastructure projects, which critics claimed increased costs and long-term financial commitments for the public sector.

6. Spin and Lack of Transparency:

- - Blair's communication strategy, which was sometimes referred to as "spin," created the impression that government decision-making lacked transparency and accountability.

7. Media Relations and Influence:

- - Blair's tight ties to media titans like Rupert Murdoch stoked doubts about the media's ability to shape public policy and eroded public confidence in the government's objectivity.

8. Activities after the Prime Minister:

- - Blair faced accusations of potential conflicts of interest and a lack of openness in his transactions as a result of his consulting job and business endeavors after leaving office.

9. The aftermath of the Iraq War

- - The continuous unrest and instability in Iraq that followed the 2003 war generated concerns about the intervention's long-term effects and its influence on the wider Middle East.

10. A breakdown in party cohesion:
- - During Blair's time as prime minister, the Labour Party had internal strife; certain sections believed that his policies led the party away from basic socialist principles.

The complexity of Blair's political legacy is reflected in these criticisms. While he was successful and contributed to modernising the Labour Party, his choices and actions also caused a great deal of controversy and continue to influence debates regarding his influence on British politics and society.

CHAPTER 9: POST POLITICAL CAREER

Tony Blair continued to be involved in international affairs after stepping down as Prime Minister of the United Kingdom in 2007. He was involved in a number of humanitarian and diplomatic projects. In order to address issues including governance, extremism, and economic growth, Blair founded the Tony Blair Institute for Global Change. Additionally, he worked on peace initiatives in the region as a Middle East ambassador for the Quartet on the Middle East. Blair's involvement in foreign issues and ongoing influence on international discussions have distinguished his post-political career.

More information on Tony Blair's post-political career is provided below:

1. The Tony Blair Institute for Global Change was established in 2016 with the goal of addressing global problems with governance, economic growth, and security. The institute's research interests include

enhancing government efficiency, preventing extremism, and fostering economic development in underdeveloped nations.

2. Blair started the "Faith and Globalization Initiative" to promote communication and understanding among various religions and civilizations. The program aims to encourage collaboration and harmonious coexistence between religious groups around the world.

3. Middle East Envoy: Blair represented the Quartet's interests in the region from 2007 until 2015. Blair's duty in the Quartet, which includes the United States, the European Union, Russia, and the United Nations, was to assist Israeli and Palestinian peace efforts. In the Palestinian territories, he tried to improve government, economic growth, and security.

4. The Tony Blair Faith Foundation is an organization that was started in 2008 with the goal of fostering religious tolerance and understanding amongst all faiths.

It sought to stop the misapplication of religion as a catalyst for violence and division.

5. Global Advisory Work: Blair offered guidance to leaders and governments all throughout the world. He provided guidance on issues of political strategy, international relations, and governance using his experience and ideas.

6. In addition to his political career, Blair also pursued entrepreneurial endeavors. He started working as a consultant and engaging in other private sector endeavors, which drew both positive and unfavorable attention because of potential conflicts of interest.

7. Public Speaking and Writing: Blair developed a reputation for his speeches in front of large crowds, frequently covering issues like world politics, the economics, and problems that the world is experiencing. He wrote books and essays on a variety of geopolitical topics, from his personal political experiences to more general ones.

8. Blair continued to be a significant presence inside the Labour Party despite his formal retirement from parliament. Media and political observers continued to seek out his comments on regional and global concerns.

9. Controversies have surfaced during Blair's post-political career. Particularly, his role in the Iraq War remained a source of discussion and criticism. While some have complimented his efforts to resolve disputes, others have criticized his involvement in certain economic ventures.

In general, Tony Blair's post-political career has been distinguished by his commitment to tackling global issues, fostering tolerance between many cultures and religions, and his continued involvement in international affairs.

9.1 Career after leaving the office

Tony Blair began a varied post-political career after stepping down as the prime minister of the United Kingdom in 2007 that was marked by a number of endeavors. Blair continues to exercise influence and participate in foreign issues, whether through international diplomacy or charitable initiatives. His post-office efforts demonstrated his dedication to solving critical global issues, fostering interfaith harmony, and influencing debates on leadership and governance. Here is a summary of Blair's post-government activities:

1. Middle East Quartet Representative:
   - - Blair took up the responsibilities of the Quartet Representative for the Middle East, which included promoting peace initiatives and encouraging economic growth in the region. His involvement demonstrated his commitment to resolving one of the most difficult and persistent disputes in the world.

Tony Blair

2. The Tony Blair Faith Foundation

- • - When he established the Tony Blair Faith
  Foundation, Blair had three goals in mind: to
  support peaceful coexistence between many
  religious traditions, promote interfaith discussion,
  and fight extremism. This action demonstrated
  his dedication to promoting tolerance and
  understanding.

3. Global Development and Philanthropy

- • - Blair established a number of institutions
  devoted to global governance and development.
  The Africa Governance Initiative sought to
  strengthen government and encourage economic
  development in African countries. The Tony
  Blair Institute for Global Change worked on
  themes like fighting extremism and improving
  government.

4. Consulting and Business Attempts:

- • - Tony Blair offered consulting services to
  governmental bodies, companies, and

organisations through the Tony Blair Associates (TBA). Although these endeavours sought to provide expertise in fields like governance and investment, they also attracted attention and criticism.

5. Public speaking and book writing:
- - Blair wrote books that offered observations on international issues and insights into his tenure as president. In his public speaking engagements, he discussed his views on leadership, world affairs, and the difficulties we face.

6. Advocacy and international problems:
- - Climate change, global health, and educational reform were just a few of the causes that Blair advocated for. He made use of his platform to push for coordinated worldwide solutions and bring attention to pressing issues.

7. The aftermath of the Iraq War

- - Blair went on to discuss the consequences of his decision to support the United States in the Iraq War. He was criticized, took part in talks regarding the effects of the war, and stood by his decisions, adding to current conversations.

8. Humanitarian efforts and Philanthropic Projects
Blair worked on humanitarian projects and programs to better the living standards, access to healthcare, and quality of education in underdeveloped areas. His initiatives demonstrated a dedication to changing people's lives for the better.

9.2 Leadership and Impact on a Global Scale

Blair's post-political actions demonstrated his sustained impact on world events, his commitment to creating positive change, and his active participation in influencing conversations about leadership, governance, and international issues.

Tony Blair's work in the post office showcased his adaptability as a statesman, advocate, and influencer on the international scene. Although his initiatives drew both praise and criticism, they demonstrated his continuous dedication to dealing with difficult problems and influencing the future on a number of fronts.

9.2 Charitable Initiatives

Tony Blair's philanthropy activities have included a variety of projects meant to address global issues, foster interfaith harmony, enhance governance, and aid in the development of underdeveloped areas. Here are some of Tony Blair's most notable charitable endeavours:

1. The Tony Blair Faith Foundation

The charity, which was established in 2008, is dedicated to fostering interfaith cooperation, understanding, and communication. Through faith-based activities, it seeks to combat extremism and create a world that is more accepting and peaceful.

2. Initiative for African Governance (AGI):
- AGI was established in 2008 with the goal of enhancing public service delivery, economic growth, and governance in African nations. Governments and the initiative work together to improve the ability of each to provide efficient policies and services.

3. Tony Blair Institute for Global Change (TBIGC):
- The institute, which was founded to study global issues and provide policy solutions, focuses on things like improving governance, thwarting extremism, and promoting economic development. It aims to have an impact on decisions that lead to constructive social transformation.

4. Advocacy for global health and development
- Blair has been a supporter of global health projects, such as attempts to fight tuberculosis and malaria. He has underlined the significance of eliminating health

inequalities and fostering access to healthcare in underdeveloped nations.

5. Youth Empowerment and Education
- Initiatives focused at enhancing educational chances for underprivileged youth are a part of Blair's humanitarian endeavors. He appreciates how education may break the cycle of poverty and promote economic development.

6. Humanitarian initiatives:
- Blair has taken part in humanitarian initiatives that benefit marginalised groups, such as refugees and internally displaced people. His actions demonstrate a dedication to reducing suffering and upholding everyone's dignity.

7. Leadership and advocacy on a global scale:
Blair has continued to use his charity activity to use his influence to address important global challenges. His advocacy encompasses issues including poverty alleviation, conflict settlement, and climate change.

8. Resolution of Conflict and Peacebuilding:
- One of Blair's priorities has been to promote peace and stability in areas that have experienced war. His participation demonstrates his dedication to settling disputes and fostering peaceful cooperation.

9. Participation with Developing Nations:
Blair's activities have primarily centered on collaborating closely with governments and leaders in developing countries to identify areas of need and provide long-term solutions for social and economic advancement.

Tony Blair's charitable activities demonstrate his dedication to having a beneficial effect on a range of international issues. He has worked to promote good change, discourse, and a more just and peaceful world through foundations, institutes, and advocacy.

9.3 Advocacy

Tony Blair's advocacy work has addressed a broad range of international concerns, demonstrating his dedication to fostering good change, overcoming difficulties, and guiding conversations on significant subjects. He has worked as an advocate in a variety of capacities, including public speaking engagements and interactions with governments and international organizations. Following are some causes Tony Blair has supported:

1. Initiatives in Global Health:
- Blair has pushed for more focus on global health challenges, including initiatives to fight tuberculosis and malaria. He underlines the significance of concerted efforts to enhance healthcare outcomes and accessibility in developing nations.

2. Action on Climate Change:
Blair has been a strong supporter of combating climate change. In order to cut carbon emissions, switch to

renewable energy sources, and lessen the effects of climate change, he has underlined the urgent need for international cooperation.

3. Youth Empowerment and Education
Blair's involvement involves pushing for universal access to high-quality education, especially in marginalized areas. He thinks that the key to social and economic advancement is education.

4. Interfaith Communication and Understanding:
Blair promotes interfaith understanding and communication through the Tony Blair Faith Foundation as a way to advance peace and fight extremism. He stresses the significance of bridging gaps across various religious groupings.

5. Resolution of Conflict and Peacebuilding:
Blair's campaigning includes pushing for amicable resolutions to disputes and supporting reconciliation in unstable areas. His involvement shows a dedication to using diplomacy to settle disputes.

6. Development and good governance
- Blair's involvement with the Tony Blair Institute for Global Change and the Africa Governance Initiative highlights his support for better governance, economic growth, and poverty reduction in developing countries.

7. "Combating Extremism":
Blair supports measures to combat extremism and radicalization. In order to stop the development of extreme ideology, he underlines the significance of resolving underlying issues and fostering societal cohesion.

8. Leadership and diplomacy on a global scale:
- Blair's advocacy highlights the importance of world leaders in resolving difficult problems. To address global concerns, he has urged intergovernmental cooperation, skillful diplomacy, and solid leadership.

9. Reduced Poverty and Social Inclusion

Tony Blair

- Blair's lobbying efforts cover issues like income inequality and supporting laws that fight poverty and encourage social inclusion. He places a strong emphasis on the necessity of inclusive economic growth for the good of all societal groups.

10. International Collaborations:
- Blair is a strong supporter of collaboration between governments, international organizations, and civil society to address global issues and advance sustainable development.

Tony Blair aims to change policy, increase awareness, and spur action on pressing global issues through his advocacy work. His involvement demonstrates his faith in the ability of group effort and leadership to bring about beneficial change on a global scale.

CONCLUSION

In "Tony Blair: The Modern Prime Minister - Navigating a New Era of Governance and Globalization," we examined the career, influence, and legacy of a politician who personified a watershed moment in British politics as well as the changing dynamics of our interconnected global community. Blair's development from a youthful, ambitious politician to a world statesman provides insightful information about the potential and challenges of a time that is changing quickly.

Blair showed a remarkable capacity to adapt and restructure the Labour Party throughout his political career, injecting it with "New Labour" ideals that sought to heal old rifts and accept contemporary realities. His inclusiveness, dedication, charismatic communication, and pragmatic leadership style dramatically altered the political scene.

Tony Blair

Blair's legacy is intricately tied to how he handled international politics. He demonstrated a leader who wanted to create a more peaceful world by his alliances with global leaders, involvement in international crises, and initiatives to advance peace-building and interfaith understanding. The book went in-depth on the intricacies of his choices, especially the Iraq War, which spurred discussions about accountability, intelligence, and action.

Blair's initiatives in the area of domestic policies attempted to update public services, improve social inclusion, and spur economic expansion. His search for the "Third Way" reflected the difficulties and aspirations of a changing society by attempting to strike a balance between market-driven policies and social responsibility.

As our investigation comes to a close, it is clear that Tony Blair left behind a legacy that includes both successes and controversies. His support for peace initiatives, global health advocacy, and educational reform demonstrate a leader who worked to make the world a better place. His involvement in conflicts and the deterioration of civil liberties at the same time created significant concerns about how to strike a balance between security and individual rights.

The book emphasises Blair's continued importance as a thought leader and advocate in a world that is getting more complex. His post-political career, which has been characterized by generosity, global leadership, and the promotion of interfaith harmony, shows his dedication to ensuring a brighter future for future generations.

The problems and goals of the modern period, which is characterized by globalization, interconnection, and the need for flexible leadership, are reflected in many ways by Tony Blair's time as prime minister. Blair's legacy serves as a reminder that leadership must be adaptable, value-driven, and conscious of the global implications of its decisions as we traverse the complexity of governance and diplomacy.

The biography "Tony Blair: The Modern Prime Minister - Navigating a New Era of Governance and

Tony Blair

Globalization" portrays the spirit of a leader who made the most of a changing world and made an enduring impact on history. As we consider his journey, we are reminded that leadership styles are as varied as the problems they seek to solve and that a leader's legacy may both challenge and inspire those who come after.